It's a Home Run, Charlie Brown!

LITTLE SIMON
An imprint of Simon & Schuster Children's Publishing Division
1230 Avenue of the Americas
New York, New York 10020

Printed in Mexico
First Edition
2   4   6   8   10   9   7   5   3   1

The Library of Congress has cataloged the paperback edition as follows:

Katschke, Judy.
It's a home run, Charlie Brown! / adapted by Judy Katschke.
p. cm. — (Ready-to-read)
"Peanuts."
"Based on the comic strips by Charles M. Schulz."
Summary: Charlie Brown is the manager of the losingest basball team in Little League.
ISBN 0-689-84939-7(pbk)
ISBN 0-689-85263-0(lib ed)
[1. Baseball—Fiction. 2. Cartoons and comics.] I. Title II. Series

PZ7.K15665 It 2002

[E]—dc21   2001038467

It's a Home Run, Charlie Brown!

Based on the comic strips
by Charles M. Schulz
Adapted by Judy Katschke
Art adapted by Nick and Peter LoBianco

Ready-to-Read

Little Simon
New York   London   Toronto   Sydney   Singapore

"It's really good to see you all here ready to begin the new baseball season," Charlie Brown said to his team. He had high hopes for them. They were going to win at least one game this year!

But in order to win, Charlie Brown's team
had to score and play better in the field. . . .

"I can't stand it!" Charlie Brown groaned
when Lucy missed the ball.

That did it! He was the manager of this
team. He was going to be tough as nails!

"Okay, Lucy," Charlie Brown said.
"Why didn't you catch that fly ball?
Let's start paying attention!"

Lucy didn't answer. She waited until
Charlie Brown turned away. Then . . .
"Bleah!"

She stuck out her tongue!

"And how about you?" Charlie Brown asked Snoopy. "You were out of position on that double play! You better look alive!"

Snoopy didn't say anything. He waited until Charlie Brown turned away. Then . . . "Bleah!"

He stuck out his tongue!

"And you sure haven't been doing much of a job behind home plate, Schroeder!" Charlie Brown complained. "How about showing some life back there?"

Schroeder didn't answer. He waited until Charlie Brown turned away. Then . . . "Bleah!"

He stuck out his tongue!

Charlie Brown walked back to the pitcher's mound. He didn't *feel* tough as nails. "Maybe I was too hard on them," Charlie Brown said to himself. "I haven't been doing too well myself. In fact, my pitching has been lousy!"

Charlie Brown realized that he had to be tough as nails on himself!

"By golly!" he said to himself. "You'd better start pitching some strikes! You'd better buckle down out here!"

Then . . .

"Bleah!"

Charlie Brown stuck out his tongue—at himself!

As the season went on, Charlie Brown's team still had not won a game. They lost the last game 123 to 0.

"Good grief!" Charlie Brown groaned. "Another ball game lost!" He felt like a loser.

"I'm tired of losing," Charlie Brown
told Lucy. "I always lose!"

Lucy felt bad for Charlie Brown. Even
blockheads need pep talks once in a while.
"Look at it this way, Charlie Brown," she
said, "we learn more from losing than we
do from winning."

Lucy was blown over backward
when Charlie Brown yelled at the top of
his lungs, "That makes me the smartest
person in the world!"
So much for pep talks!

But the next game, Charlie Brown's team had a good chance to win. The score was three to three in the bottom of the ninth.

"I can't look!" Lucy said. She covered her eyes and groaned.

Suddenly Lucy realized her teammates were excited.

"We already have two outs!" Lucy said.

"But Charlie Brown is on third," Patty explained. "And our best hitter is coming up!"

Lucy looked at Charlie Brown standing on third base. Then she had a terrible thought. . . .

"You don't think Charlie Brown will try to steal home?" Lucy asked. "Do you?"

Patty shook her head. "Never!" she said. "Not even Charlie Brown would do anything *that* stupid!"

Meanwhile, on third base . . .

I wonder if I should try to steal home, Charlie Brown thought. If he scored a run, his team would win! And he would be a hero!

Charlie Brown pictured the whole thing. His team would carry him on their shoulders. They would even cheer his name!

I have to try it! Charlie Brown thought. If I'm going to be a hero, I have to steal home! As he inched away from the plate he mapped out his plan in his head.

"First I'll dance around a little on the baseline," Charlie Brown said to himself. "That will confuse the pitcher!"

Charlie Brown hopped to the left. He hopped to the right.

"And then I'll . . ."

Charlie Brown looked over his shoulder.

The ball was whizzing toward the batter at home plate!

"Take off!" Charlie Brown shouted.

His friends went wild! They all cheered for good ol' Charlie Brown!

"Charlie Brown is trying to steal home! Slide, Charlie Brown, slide!" they shouted.

Charlie Brown slid in a cloud of dust.
But he didn't mind. Happiness was stealing
home and winning the game! And becoming
a hero at last!

But when Charlie Brown skidded to a stop, he didn't get a hero's welcome.

"Oh, you blockhead!" Lucy shouted.

Charlie Brown gulped. Did she say—'blockhead'?

"Am I out?" Charlie Brown asked.

Lucy glared down at Charlie Brown. "Out?!" Lucy shouted. "You blockhead. You didn't even get halfway home!"

He wasn't a hero. He was just a goat . . . as usual. And as he lay on the field until dark, all Charlie Brown could say was . . . "Rats!"

The season ended without a single win.
"I'm glad the baseball season is over," Charlie Brown told Linus. "I don't ever want to hear the word 'baseball' again. I think if I hear the word 'baseball' again, I'll scream!"

Linus looked carefully at Charlie Brown.
"Baseball," he said.

"Aaaugh!" Charlie Brown screamed.

But he didn't mean it. Maybe his team *had* lost every game of the season. None of that mattered, because they could try again next year!

PLAY BALL!